Riding the Wheel

Riding the Wheel

prose-poems

Peter Anderson

© 2024 Peter Anderson. All rights reserved.
This material may not be reproduced in any form, published,
reprinted, recorded, performed, broadcast,
rewritten, or redistributed without
the explicit permission of Peter Anderson.
All such actions are strictly prohibited by law.

Cover design by Shay Culligan
Cover art by Bulgarian artist Gergana Yordanova
Author photo by Citrus Anderson

ISBN: 978-1-63980-592-1

Kelsay Books
502 South 1040 East, A-119
American Fork, Utah 84003
Kelsaybooks.com

For my family,
for my friends,
and for many fine years
in the San Luis Valley.

Acknowledgments

Thanks to the editors of the publications listed below who published earlier versions of writings in this book:

Crestone Eagle: Everything except the haikus
Colorado Central Magazine: Everything except the haikus
Deep Wild Journal: "Party Animals," "Riding the Wheel"
Heading Home: Field Notes (Conundrum Press/Bower House Books): "Mountain Time"

Contents

Ground of Being	11
Winter	14
Mountain Time	16
Inside the Ice House	17
The Cosmic Highway	18
Hope in the Stars	19
Spring	22
Postcards to Blanca Peak	24
Arockalypse	26
The Case of the Man-Eating Dune	27
Haibun for a Cool Trail	29
Summer	32
Some Creekside Meditations on Moving Water	34
Row, Row, Row	36
Dreaming the Map	38
Good News from the Higher Elevations	39
Fall	42
Gleaning	44
Party Animals	45
Spanish Trail	46
The Man Who Slept with a Bear	49
Riding the Wheel	53

Ground of Being

1. The Ute name for the Great Sand Dunes is *sowapophe-uvehe*—the land that goes back and forth. The Jicarilla Apache call it *ei-enyedi*—the land that goes up and down. On a windy spring day that belongs to the dust devils and tumbleweeds, either name might apply to the entire San Luis Valley. It is a good day to lay low, if you can, and give thanks for shelter.

Shelter, though, is a relative term. Today, I put on my mask and gloves and went hunting and gathering downtown—socially distancing down the aisles of the Mercantile in pursuit of a few groceries. As I left the store, I noticed someone laid out on a bench across the street, seeking a little respite from the wind on the lee side of a backpack crammed full of stuff.

If I were at loose ends, maybe I too would come here. I can see how a little town at the end of the road would appeal to those who are weary of navigating a viral urban landscape. I hear comments—mostly meant facetiously (sometimes less so by preppers and those expecting an apocalypse)—about barricading the only road into town in the event of widespread chaos, which reminds me of a story about a village where some of the locals were building bomb shelters. A boy asked his father why he wasn't building one. "Because," his father said, "I don't want to be in the position of closing the door on one of our neighbors if we don't have enough space or food for them too."

2. One week into the pandemic, a woman doing errands decided to steer clear of the post office and all the chatter there. She'd heard so many prayers, proclamations, and conspiracy theories, not to mention all the prognosticators who were making predictions on the duration of the quarantine, that she decided to walk to the chapel where hardly anyone went anymore. She sat on the old

wooden bench, looking up through the cobwebs spanning the window behind the altar, and enjoyed the changing light as the afternoon clouds came and went.

The retired cop showed up at the firehouse and asked if there was anything he could do. The fireman added the cop's name to a list of volunteers for an emergency response team and took down his phone number. We'll call you, he said. Ok, but is there anything I can do right now, the cop wondered? Well, we did have an old guy call in a few minutes ago who needed some groceries, the fireman said, as he handed over the list: toilet paper, Purex, oatmeal, Maxwell House coffee, Saltines, and prunes. When he got to the grocery store, the cop found the shelves empty where the toilet paper and Purex should have been. He wondered if the old man liked his prunes dry or canned.

The parents were exhausted. Their boys, who had been going to school via their laptops for several days, were fighting constantly. One afternoon, they all went outside to walk the dogs who were already headed up the trail though the ponderosas. "Better go catch up," said the father. The nine-year-old took off running, the seven year-old did his best to keep up, and the parents followed. After a while they saw the boys and the dogs in a clearing up ahead. The two old mutts were prancing around like puppies as the boys gave chase. "That's what we used to call runnin' your stink off," said the mom.

The poet lit a candle and sat down at her desk. How strange, she thought, that in this time of "social distancing," she felt more connected than ever with the rest of humanity. She took a dollar bill out of her wallet and held it under the light. Whose hands had touched it before her own, she wondered? A carrier of the virus? Or just a neighbor? She chose the latter.

3. Downtown, I noticed several license plates from the Lone Star State. Given the choice during a pandemic, or any other time for that matter, I wouldn't stay put in Houston or Dallas either. But choice is the key word. Many people have no choice but to stay put, even if "put" isn't a great situation. Others have a choice but can't narrow it down to one place. Unrelenting wind and dust in the spring, clouds of mosquitos a few months later, high fire danger in a dry year—some might wonder why anyone would live here, but this end-of-the-road place has been good to me. I do better when I can see a lot of sky, when I can watch the weather come and go, when I can share a little more elbow room with my neighbors, many of whom are wild and four-legged.

Here on the edge of the Sangre de Cristos, east is wild and steep, west is open and rural, and north and south consist of public and therefore mostly uninhabited common lands. Your place may be a good place to shelter for some of the same reasons: mountains, public lands, and a community where you know your neighbors. This place has given me all of that, as it has given me the words that follow.

Winter

                    wind-feathered cloud drifts
                    east, westbound moon, a buoy
                    in this sea of sky

on this birthday walk,
hundreds of gifts—a river
of elk headed south

just below the sky,
slag, crag, and crevice—
only the snow stays.

                    blue grama shadow—
                    crescent seedhead, a new moon
                    tethered to the snow

skiing through low cloud
flat light, legs feel for the slope
that the eyes can't read.

                        rice grass quivers here—
                        on the ridge, spindrift plumes
                        into azure sky.

                        walking my own tracks—
                        snow, road, distant yellow bus
                        fifty years from here

flashy birds long gone,
but you're still singing
chickadee-dee-dee.

Mountain Time

Imagine this beginning: a molecule rides in your own exhale, water in the form of vapor, rising in a warmer stream of air to meet the cooler floor of a cloud, a cloud that the prevailing wind has nudged up against the western slope of a nearby mountain. Inside of the cloud, let's say this molecule, once a part of your own being, bumps into a grain of a grain of a grain of sand. And let's say some other water molecules mingling nearby drift into that same particle. Pretty soon, all those molecules, including your own, are linking up like star-to-the-right square dancers on a Saturday night.

Out in the valley, a trucker sits next to a window at a roadside café. He clears a circle of vapor, his own breath in part, to look out the window. Clouds are piling up on the mountain. The good news: he's headed over the lowest pass leaving the valley. The bad news: the curves are always in the shadows up there. "I hate being on that road when it gets slick," he says to the waitress. "What kind of pie d'you say you had?"

Nearby a rancher hauling hay rattles across a frozen brown pasture in an old flatbed. As he listens to the snow advisory on the radio, he takes a pull off a Pall Mall and blows out a puff of blue smoke. Bring it on, he says to himself. Then he recalls snow drifts over fences and his whole herd spread out from hell to breakfast down County Road T.

Back on the slope of the mountain the snow is falling. You see a doe nudging her two fawns toward the shelter of a pinyon. Is it the wind chill of the gust that just caught you head-on or is the temperature falling fast? You find the answer on the black sleeve of your wool shirt. What fell as pellets of hail only a few minutes ago now falls in the form of six-winged lattices, lovely translucent crystals which linger as long it takes your exhaled breath to disappear.

Inside the Ice House

Lately we have been wrapped in clouds. They like to linger along the western flanks of the mountain. Shadows, which we saw reaching further north as the sun went south, must have left for the Arctic, taking with them the contours they usually reveal. If it weren't for the rabbit brush poking up through the snow, we would have no way to measure our movement in this flat light. The high peaks have ventured off beyond our quilted fog to reinvent themselves. We will not be able to ignore their new shine when they return, but today the colors that usually dazzle us here are muted. For a while we can let our eyes rest. In this ice house of an inversion, green thinks it might like to become gray for a while. And why not? Maybe, as we kick and glide, kick and glide, and follow our skis down the old ranch road to Deadman Creek, we will turn the color of winter like the weasels do and become invisible against a horizon newly dusted with snow.

The Cosmic Highway

In a winter inversion, when a layer of cold air traps the vapors rising from high desert wetlands, the visions begin. A few miles away, buildings in the tiny town of Moffat soar into the sky as if part of Manhattan has been transplanted overnight. San Antonio Mountain, 100 miles to the south, appears to be floating over the valley. Distance here, both vast and visible, has its way with you. Beware the hypnotic effect of the powerline poles that punctuate the roadside skyline, drawing your gaze toward a distant vanishing point. Pull over if you feel drowsy. Otherwise you may be transported through time and space into the lane of an oncoming semi or, like me, you may beam across that lane altogether, and wake up with the chico and rabbitbrush slapping at your bumper. At night there are ghosts, like the coyote you clip with your right fender. When you approach the carcass to pull it off the road, it rises up resurrected and skedaddles through a barbed wire fence. Sometimes you're not sure where you are—is this Mosca or Hooper coming up?—or if you will ever get there, wherever there may be. It's as if the spaces between these little towns are elastic or maybe you're just experiencing the expanding nature of the universe itself. Will this cosmic highway ever end? On a moonless winter night, when you see a long straight road and nothing but stars up ahead, as if you could drive by Polaris, the North Star, and right up the handle of the Little Dipper, it really doesn't matter.

Hope in the Stars

"I know nothing with any certainty," he said, "but the sight of the stars always makes me dream." And it was a good thing they did. Without that river of light coursing through the blue-black sky, he had only his work. Painting was distraction enough for a while. But he could only put in so many hours. And even then he wasn't able to lose himself deeply enough to avoid those horrible fits of anxiety that surged through his being like an electrical storm. Nor could he avoid the emptiness and the fatigue that left him unable to function and drove him back to bed in a small room on the second floor. Thank God for the window. And the hills. And above them the river of the great beyond.

There is so much more to the Milky Way than the light reveals. Those spaces between the stars aren't empty after all, but that was an understanding that came long after his time. He wouldn't have known then that the weightiness of those dark places contained "brown dwarfs"—hunks of matter that weren't big enough to start burning—or "white dwarfs"—the remnant cores of burnt out stars—or "black holes"—the collapsed mass that remains after stars explode. He wouldn't have known about dark matter, that light-bending mass between the stars whose source we have yet to fully fathom.

As he looked out the portal from his second story garret, it occurred to him that the night was more richly colored than the day. Such an observation might be lost on casual observers, but those who were willing to ride those trails of vision further into the night could not help but notice intense waves of violet, blue, and green. And then there were the stars themselves . . . they were so much more than white dots on a blue-black dome. "If only you pay attention," he said, "you will see that certain stars are lemon-yellow, others pink or a green blue," all of them shining with "forget-me-not brilliance."

The night sky is different now than it was in his time. If he were looking out his garret window tonight, he would not be able to see the Milky Way as we are able to see it here on the edge of the Sangre de Cristos. Too many lights. Stranger still, he would find out that more than a third of the earth's inhabitants are similarly deprived of the vibrant night sky that had once been his obsession. Other than scattered rural populations, as well as those who study the stars with high-powered telescopes, most people have settled into the neon conveniences of the nearby and care less about the darker mysteries of the faraway—the same mysteries that would call him back, time and again, to the great "starlit vault of heaven."

"Hope," he said, "is in the stars." And for a tormented soul like him, hope was a matter of survival. It was the promise of liberation, at least temporarily, from the psychic weather he referred to as the "storm within." It may be hard for us to fathom the kind of suffering that ultimately caused him to take his own life. Then again, maybe not. For those of us who have weathered a few rough patches, maybe it's just a matter of degree. Maybe that's why we are drawn to the swirling starry night Van Gogh rendered so beautifully several months before his death in 1889. Or why we look forward to the company of all our stars during this dark season as Jupiter and Saturn ride off at dusk, side-by-side, toward the western edge of the sky.

Spring

                fast moving storm cloud
                windblown beads of graupel, white
                over tawny grass

morning snowmelt, sand
still damp—walking the road
where the water ran

from their window sill
lookout, two cats spying on
birds and tumbleweeds

                today the treetops,
                as if at an all-night rave,
                dance, dance, dance, and dance.

crown of light over
a gap in the ridge—bearing
the moon on the mountain

        drifting veils of rain,
        distant lightning, an old fencepost
        and a meadowlark's song

        barbed wire tumble-
        weed, you almost got away—
        better luck next time.

last light on the snowfields,
alpenglow, the range gone red—
Sangre de Cristo

Postcards to Blanca Peak

1. Dear Blanca,

On this postcard we see you from the north. The clouds have saddled up on your high ridges, where, for a while, they will stay, until they realize you're not going anywhere. Then they'll get restless. "I'm gonna get me a ride on the wind and head out to the prairie," one of them says, ". . . maybe see what Dodge City ain't got." Others will follow. Clouds roll like that.

2. Dear Blanca,

This postcard pictures you as photographed by the Wheeler Survey who put you on an early map. They were among the first to make your summit. But someone, a hunter perhaps, had already made a wall of stone up there, maybe for shelter, maybe for protection, maybe to render themselves invisible to their enemies or their prey. Who knows? You do.

3. Dear Blanca,

The photo on this postcard must have been taken somewhere up in the South San Juans looking east. Your looming presence shines underneath a cloudless sky. It is not hard to imagine, from this vantage point, how you would have made a huge impression on the Diné people who came into this valley from the west. No wonder you found a way onto their maps of the sacred. They say First Man and First Woman brought you up from the underworld and fastened you to this ground with rainbows and lightning bolts. We are reminded of this when the summer storms come.

4. Dear Blanca,

This postcard shows some mountaineers approaching you from Lake Como. We know the clouds get restless, but you move too. People who know their rocks tell us you are young and still growing, though not enough for most of us to notice. But when we are climbing your talus, we realize you are anything but sedentary. We take two steps up and you take one step back. Sometimes, we think we are closing in on your summit, but then we lose sight of it. The next time we see it, that part of you is not where we thought it was. Are you trying to avoid us?

Arockalypse

Here along the Rio Grande Rift, our planet's outer crust looks solid enough, but really it is thin and taut and ready, after centuries of pent-up geo-tension, for a shimmy-shakin' bump & grind. Today I walk underneath my home, past its flimsy cinder block piers. If this land were to up and buck itself out from underneath us, would this old house ride it out? Would the beams crack? Would the roof hold? Duck and cover, baby. Once, in a different home, the geological hand we held was much worse, since the fault we lived on was fourteen hundred years into a fourteen-hundred-year gap (give or take a few centuries) between foothill shakedowns. Every afternoon the ten-story apartment building next door cast its queen-of-spades shadow on our little house. Here on the Rio Grande Rift it's been 7,500 years since the last big deal went down, but arockalypse only happens here every fifteen thousand years (give or take a few centuries). So I'll lean back in my ho-hum chair, chum, and make a run with a full house. Let the cards fall as they may.

The Case of the Man-Eating Dune

Had it gone another way, forensics might have revealed the fragment of a button from a dress shirt, the metal frame of the eyeglasses, the strip of leather from the handle of a book bag, the shredded textbook cover—a title having something to do with imaginative writing, all of which might suggest an English professor. Digital analysis of the car radio would have revealed that the driver had been tuned into a public radio station. Given the unending wave of Trumpian headlines at the time of burial, it may have been a suicide. Why else would someone drive a low-riding Mazda into a sand dune during a severe wind storm? Must have been a troubled democrat.

As it happened, I was headed into Hooper when I found out that poor visibility and an accident had closed off the highway headed north. Hoping to drive around the road closure, I turned west into a dust cloud. That's when the short cut occurred to me. Why go all the way west to Highway 285? Why not head north on one of the many farm roads that run up the center of the valley? Wind and sand, that's why. But I wasn't thinking about that as I turned north onto a dirt road and drove off into the apocalypse. It wasn't an apocalypse at first. I passed a sign that said "No County Road Maintenance Beyond This Point"—don't worry, be happy—and kept driving north. That's when everything beyond my windshield began to drift in an easterly direction. Once visible road ruts in the sand soon vanished. Only a nit-witted, knuckleheaded numbskull would continue. I put the pedal to the metal. And I drove into a recently formed dune. That's when I heard the Lord speak: "Better dig your ass out pretty quick." It was all I could do to open the door against the prevailing wind. Part of the dune flew in before I could close it behind me. My front tires were still visible. Just barely. I swept armfuls of sand away until I could see the hubcaps—Progress!—and kept flailing away until I was able to rock that little Mazda around and drive away from the beast. But it followed me all the way back to the blessed asphalt of Highway 17, where I cranked a hard left, ditched the dune, and put the hammer down for County Road T—there's no place like home . . . there's no place like home . . . there's no place like home.

Haibun for a Cool Trail

I am looking at a diagram of neural pathways in the brain, the way they meander—dipping and turning and looping back on themselves. A favorite trail near my house moves across the mountain that way. Maybe that's why I find it so pleasing. Or maybe it's just because it is an anomaly here on the western flank of the Sangre de Cristos, where most of the trails are intent on taking you straight up the mountain. This trail, which surfs the contours running north-south along the alluvial edge of the range, is not ambitious. It would rather dawdle in the pinyons and junipers and admire the ponderosas that have found a home on the edge of their range. It would rather pause for a long extended gaze out over the valley where the cottonwoods carry the last flash of yellow brilliance before the winds of November take it all away. It will gain some elevation, but only because it enjoys making some wide turns down the mountain shortly thereafter. This trail doesn't draw attention to itself. It doesn't have to announce itself with a parking lot and a bulletin board. Its manner of seduction isn't "Hey mister, you lookin' for a good time?" It offers only the first hint of a smile. Here you register with your feet as they follow a curling path of sand into the arroyo where an old homesteader of a ponderosa has been living the good life, its deep roots welcoming the waters that visit from time to time. Further along, the trail is a ribbon of sand winding through a wide patch of prickly pear. Then you pass a huge anthill, one of many along the trail, which remind you of the scientist who discovered their path-making secret—an obscure gland which releases pheromonal trail blazes that tell the other ants, "Yes, this is a good way, walk in it." And they would be right . . . this is a good way. Sometimes, if you walk along watching your feet as they navigate this meandering trail, you may fall into some pinyon-juniper dreamtime, where the entire world is gray, green and tawny, until you round a bend and wake up to the brilliant red blast of the appropriately named skyrocket gilia, a wild bloom that would delight any hummingbird. This trail dips and rises, rolls and loops like the lilting wraparound notes of Paul Desmond's saxophone in "Take Five," the Brubeck Quartet classic. There is nothing harsh or discordant here—this is a cool jazz kind of trail. Even when it turns uphill, it meanders, slack-rope looping here and there, around a juniper and through an opening between two pinyons, flowing, sure, but with a recurring theme, as if in sync with Brubeck's piano chords—the ones that repeatedly bring you home to the core melody—while your feet are tap-tap-tapping out Joe Morello's rhythm on symbol and snare, and Eugene Wright is holding a steady pulse on the bass as up the hill you go, until you break out into a clearing, pausing to savor what follows.

Rabbitbrush holds on
to the last light, then gives it
up to the mountain.

Summer

        welcome back hermit
        thrush, your song fills the hole
        you left in the sky.

mountain sun rising
sweeps up valley shadows
the night left behind.

falcon on a spruce
snag preening, a feather
floating on the breeze

              walking the switchbacks—
              empty head, what happened
              to all your noise?

inside looking out
eclipse of the sky—dog's nose
in a gopher hole

                such a small puddle
                carries trees clouds and moon
                all rippled in sky.

            scars left behind
            by old aspen branches, eyes
            upon the world

    uphill, I carry
    food water shelter—downhill
    the mountain carries me.

Some Creekside Meditations on Moving Water

1. In the everyday shade where the horsetails grow, a white wave washes-washes-washes over a fallen tree. The letter "s" is shaped like a meander of moving water and sounds like steam rushing through a kettle spout. Right here anyway, "S" is this creek's favorite letter. Yes, Yes, Yes. But that "S" likes to make music—splashh-shooshh-shooshh-splashh—wherever it can find an "H" or two to run with. This is what the creek has to say. But wait. There's more. Little waves that murmur through quiet shallows gurgle and slurp onto the ground below your feet.

2. When there is more snow up high, the creek has a daily pulse. You can hear it if you listen in the morning and then listen again in the afternoon. When the sun peeks over the ridge and morning light floods the shadowy nooks and crannies where the snow still lives, tiny streams find their way down through the talus, and join thousands of other tiny streams on their way down the mountain, and the creek will welcome them and rise as it does, and whatever it was singing in the morning, it will sing louder in the afternoon.

3. For the dipper—the "hummingbird of blooming waters," as John Muir once wrote—moving water is social security. Let it rush and ripple. Let it foam and foment. Wherever the fast water flowers forth, the dipper knows there will be insects—mayflies, midges, and mosquitoes. Tired of the same old bugs? Try the underwater menu: dragonfly nymphs, caddisfly larvae, maybe some baby crawfish. Looking for a home away from annoying neighbors? High ledge, waterfall spray, rainbows in the afternoon shine. Views. Views. Views. No wonder the dipper is always bursting into song.

4. This creek sings doo-wop mostly: Shah-Shah-Shalang-alang. If you sit beside it long enough, you may want a watery word that carries a little more meaning. How about sashay? It has a watery sound to it, and even seems to suggest some watery characteristics. To sashay is to "proceed in a casual manner," to "flounce in a showy manner," or to "move in a sideways manner." This creek has manners and does it all. Then you think of sashaying square dancers, how they circle around one another like the swirling currents in an eddy, and somehow you feel just a little bit closer to the everyday downward dance that is this water on a summer day.

5. What if a water molecule could tell you where it's been? *I been away down deep on the ocean floor, surfed a big tsunami, rode a thunderhead to Yellowstone, settled in a geyser and come out with Old Faithful, rode the Snake into Idaho and down the mighty Columbia, holed up in a fog bank over the Olympic pee-ninsula, which finally rained me into the Pacific where I got swallered by an orca whale who spouted me out off the coast of Mexico, where I come in with the tide and hitched a ride on a northwester up through Arizonee, across the Great Divide, and over the valley on a monsoon cloud that landed me in the Sangrees, where I stayed put on a high ridge cause I liked it some, till I froze up when it all turned cold and stayed the winter, and now I'm a-surfin' the thaw and whoo-whee you just never know . . .*

And then the rest of the creek says what it says so well:
Hush. Hush. Hush.

Row, Row, Row

For Atlas

Row, row, row your boat. Row it because El Rio is running high with water that has just come down off the mountain and your friends want to take their little boy on his first float; row it so he feels the waves as they push up against the floor of the raft, so that a small wave over the bow will surprise him—yes, this water still carries its high snow chill; row it so he can see how the river gives itself away, parting ways around an island, then gathering itself up into swirls and eddies on the far side; row it because even in a bulky craft like this, you may feel like a water strider gliding across the current; row it so that he will see the merganser floating along beside the boat before she paddles into lift-off and flies downstream; row it for his smile as she takes flight.

Gently down the stream. It is good to float and drift and let the river guide you. Let it tell you where you need to be. Let it slide you across the riffles and around the pillow of water above a submerged boulder. Yes, this river can rock—last week you rode the big waves in that narrow whitewater canyon upstream—but here it rolls like an up-tempo bossa nova. Let it remind you that there is no need to hurry, just a little dip of the oar here and there, so that you are moving with most of the current, which will deliver you in due time to your destination a few miles downstream.

Merrily, merrily, merrily, merrily. Because on a day like today, as the old rat told his Wind-in-the-Willow friends, "There is nothing . . . half so much worth doing as messing about in boats." The river carries you for free—oooh-whee, ride me high—and your blue boat glides though sun-splash and refracted sky. Gravity invites you to hitch a ride for as long as you want, and you think, why not, let's roll all the way to the delta where the ocean has been waiting for the river, tapping its toes in the sand: "It's about time you came home." Here now on this boat, both mother and father are attentive to their little boy and whatever his floating reveries may be.

Life is but a dream. You arrive at your destination much sooner than expected and you barely catch the eddy. Now you pull your boat onto the shore, sit under the shade of a willow, and look back at the river that has delivered you to this grassy oasis where the little boy's mom is preparing lunch. What will her two-year-old remember from this day? What is he thinking now as you sit on the boat and look back up the river? Someday, maybe he will find out that you can hear the river anywhere if you cup your hands over your ears because the river runs through us. Today you tap, tap, tap, the tip of the oar on the bow of the blue raft, keeping time as you teach him, in call-and-response fashion, a song you learned a long time ago:

Row, row, row, your boat . . .
Woe-woe-woe-yer-boe . . .
Gently down the stream.
Went-we-down-da-weam.
Merrily, Merrily, Merrily, Merrily.
Mary-mary-mary-mary.
Life is but a dream.
Lie-da-dee-da-dweem.

Dreaming the Map

I had been everywhere in the Road Atlas except for Alabama and Mississippi, but I had used those pages for fire starter, so I was looking for a new state and I found it one night in my secret life— new territory where colorful fishing dories were floating the headwaters of a river that disappeared into a deep canyon several miles downstream. It had just rained, so I rolled down the window and inhaled the heady aroma of wet sage. I drove into a college town nestled into the tanned foothills of an unfamiliar mountain range. A local radio announcer said that a wolf pack was forming on the edge of town and the Nez Pierce were holding a pow wow down by the fairgrounds. I was thinking about becoming a student again—maybe signing up for a seminar called "The Drifter in American Literature"—and getting to know a student body made up of hardy fifth generation mountain girls who were highly interested in newcomers. I never did find the registrar and had no idea when classes started, so I bought a vanilla shake from a roller-skating cowgirl down at the Tastee Freeze, and drove some inviting dirt roads into the hills until I took one that left the valley but did not return. Never have been able to find my way back, but that's as it should be. Any map needs a promised land whose secrets we may never know.

Good News from the Higher Elevations

I am here, brothers and sisters, to testify to the wilderness cure. Yes, brothers and sisters, I have been healed, once again, in the First Church of the Higher Elevations. Hallelujah! Can I get a witness?   Healed from what, you may ask? I have been healed, brothers and sisters, from the existential swamp that is the pandemic blues. Healed from the old black dog of perpetual and chronic melancholia brought on by the state of our nation and the planet on which it stands. Healed from the incessant miasma of yammering yay-hoo's on social media and elsewhere. Healed from the mind-numbing diversions that we call news and entertainment. Healed from the noise that inhabits the daily static, which passes for thought inside our heads.   Yes, Friends, I'm here to tell you, salvation awaits out yonder in the First Church of the Higher Elevations. Out where the last of the twisted timbers grow, and beyond to the rocks and tundra where the pikas eek eek eek out their living, where higher still the great storm clouds are born and where their waters fall and part ways on the Great Divide. Amen, brothers and sisters, can I get a witness?   Yes, Friends, I have shed the heavy burden of the pandemic pounds that came in the form of frozen delights I could not resist in gas station coolers; that came in the guise of ice-filled libations on hot summer evenings which promised and delivered momentary peace, but which ultimately added to the freight that this old carcass must bear in the navigation of the day-to-day. I know you know the burden of which I speak, which resides in the guise of incessant temptation from every direction. This is our collective burden to bear, Friends, but today I want to testify to the liberation I have known after ten days of meager provisions—pitiful rations of ramen, freeze-dried fruit, miso soup, maybe a few nuts, just enough to fuel the biological engine that can carry one up another thousand feet. Blessed is the wife who provides this humble nourishment. Yea, it is the manna that will lead one further into the promised land.

Amen. Hallelujah.   Yes, Friends, I have suffered through the inevitable journey into the night, the humbling but very necessary exit from sleeping bag and tent into the depths of the darkness, following the battered beam of light thrown from one's own head into the high meadows where one may relieve oneself of the heavy bladdered burdens that we try and deny well into the early morning hours, and I am here to tell you that the rewards are great, Friends, and that the heavens themselves will sing out with all their streaking Perseid lights, which I witnessed as I stood there humbled in little more than my own birth suit. Hallelujah.   Make no mistake, Friends, there will be other trials in the First Church of the Higher Elevations. Perhaps you will have to endure the blight of the small winged ones, clouds of which will torment you with their persistent whining and unending desire to celebrate a wilderness communion with your very blood. Again and again, you will have to bear the burden of gravity as you begin another ascension up the switchbacks into the higher realms. You will curse those places where the trees fall across your trail, where you are forced to take long detours in order to find your way forward again, but as the prophet Ecclesiastes says, "If a tree falls to the south or to the north, in the place where the tree falls, there it will lie."   The "it" that he refers to is, of course, the kingdom which awaits all of us, which in fact surrounds us here in the headwaters region of our fair state. You need only head out past the town of Couldbe, further and higher past the Whynot Campground, and yonder still to the trailhead that leads into the Wherefore Wilderness, where one step and then another will ultimately lead you into the presence that awaits us all in the First Church of the Higher Elevations.

Excelsior.

Fall

                    dude who shot the o's
                    out of the "no shooting" sign
                    got more lead than brains.

silence-wind, raven
adds an exclamation point,
a mountain sentence.

cedar post corral,
all the old wire down, how long
have your cows been gone?

                    if I could only
                    have one sky all year . . . blue
                    with yellow aspens.

hey ponderosa,
are you playing the wind or
does the wind play you?

six bucks run the hill—
the last one lingers, then turns
to see who's coming.

last light cottonwood,
only a keen eye can tell
the owl from the branch.

driving north, nothing
but sand, clay, and rabbitbrush
and then a white cross

Gleaning

Somewhere in the Bible, he recalls, the farmers leave the remnants of their harvest for the hungry. It is still so for those who know where to look. As the high aspens begin to turn, the sandhill cranes circle above the valley before settling into some shallow wetlands down by the dunes. They will spend the night there, safe from predators. Early in the morning, they will fly west across the valley to glean the leftover grains from vacant farm fields. In a few days, he will rattle by those same fields in a beat-up Chevy with New Mexico plates, scanning a dusty county road for russets jostled loose as the big potato trucks ride the ruts and bumps toward a warehouse in Monte Vista. He likes to come north as the cranes rest and feed here before flying south to winter in the warmer valleys of the Rio Grande. Like them, he knows he will find food. And as the first snow dusts the high Sangre de Cristo peaks, he camps along the western edge of the range, burning pinyon and juniper until he has a nice bed of coals. He wraps a few potatoes in tin foil and lays them in the fire. Later he peels back their blackened silver jackets, slits them open, and slathers them with butter. And he gives thanks for the humble mountain tuber, first tasted high in the Andes, now harvested in this mountain valley—Purple Peruvian, Colorado Rose, Rio Grande Russet. Tomorrow morning, he will drive home to Espanola. In a couple of weeks the cranes will follow. And he will hear them before he sees them as they emerge from some low storm clouds over the river.

Party Animals

I must have missed one of the rock cairns that marked the trail and walked off the map, but I did find a fine camp in a high meadow. An island of spruce shielded me from elk grazing through the waning tundra light in a snow-rimmed cirque a mile or so off toward the Divide. If my inner compass was a little off, so what? This was a good place to be lost. As the elk herd approached, a slight breeze came down with them, floating my scent off toward the sun which had gone down behind a distant ridge. As far as the elk were concerned I wasn't there. Even when the walls of my tent billowed out in an occasional puff of wind, I didn't exist. So they came closer and closer and soon I could hear the cows and calves mewing and bleating to one another on the far side of the spruce. Right around dusk, I saw something strange. Two cows got up on their hind legs and faced off toward one another, hooves pressed chest to chest, not in an aggressive way, but more like a dance, a kind of wapiti-style cha-cha-cha. A friend once told me he had witnessed elk sliding down a snow field for no apparent reason other than their own amusement. It wasn't long after the full moon had risen, that I noticed another curious behavior. Over on the edge of the meadow, a cow elk kicked an unidentifiable moonlit object into the air and then jumped back as if she had startled herself with the sparkle of it all. Then she did it again. And again. And then a few more curious cows came over to see what was going on and joined in on the action. I watched them through the skeeter-mesh wall of my tent until I was too tired to hold my head up any longer. That's when I zipped up my sleeping bag, the sound of which spooked the whole herd. They vanished into the trees and shadows, leaving me to ponder the dreamy scene I had just witnessed. The next morning, if only to get a grip on what was real and what wasn't, I moseyed out into the meadow looking for evidence of the previous night's follies and found the remains of a deflated tinfoil balloon. The elk were long gone. So was their piece of the moon.

Spanish Trail

Today, under a gray sky, the wind carries the lingering cold, the first fires of the season burn in woodstoves downtown, and there is only one other car parked out by the cemetery—someone eating lunch with the heater running. The map I've been studying tells me I am following the northern branch of the old Spanish Trail. Out here there are pinyons, junipers, and ponderosas old enough to have witnessed those caravans of horses, mules, and traders passing through. Back then, it would have taken a couple dozen riders to keep as many as 200 mules moving in the right direction. On this day, it's just the dog and me headed out on a sandy two-track north of town.

> Eastbound storm clouds,
> only the crow heads west
> across the valley.

Wabi-sabi, something the great haiku poet Basho understood and appreciated, is the name for a Japanese approach to the beauties of this world, which values qualities related to three ideas: nothing lasts, nothing is finished, and nothing is perfect. Wabi-sabi celebrates flaws and imperfections, even the sign out here, full of rusted bullet holes, that says "No Shooting." It is at home in this high desert, where the wind throttles these old pinyons and junipers, some of which are bent and gnarled and barely hanging on and have been that way for centuries. It is alive and well in an abandoned stock tank. It finds a home in the dessicated graininess of an old cedar fence post. The idea that beauty thrives in the process of decay, that the prospect of an object's demise enhances its radiant appeal, offers comfort to someone my age, so often reminded that time is tight and getting tighter every day.

> Rusted wire fenceline
> spliced here, pulled taut there,
> those old hands long gone

Today, as the dog retrieves a bone or two from this drifting sand, I wonder about everything else that is buried out here. I think about the artifacts—musket balls, bridle bits and spurs, tin cups and water flasks, hunting knives, brass buttons that came in handy as trade items with the Utes. I think about those who left them behind. Like the elk whose trails reflect a desire for cover, food, and water, these trail riders would have appreciated the stealth and shelter offered by a few fully grown trees. They might have enjoyed the bounty of some pinyon nuts. They depended on the occasional creek to water themselves and their animals. Though much wider than the contemporary trails we follow into the high country, their trail, at least around here, was limited to the relatively narrow corridor that offered these amenities. They camped in the midst of what are now old growth pinyons and junipers. If their wayfaring spirits linger anywhere, surely one would find them here.

> Though we have not met
> you and I are travelers
> along this sandy road.

I am not a hunter, gatherer, or trader. So what is the desire line I am following on this trail headed north along the edge of the valley? It has to do with some small, or maybe not so small, pleasures—watching the weather, enjoying the often-ignored miracle of a functioning body, bearing witness to the slow turning of a brain liberated from its quotidian responsibilities—all of which are nurtured by the absence of everything that makes noise in our lives.

Even the jays are quiet.
In this field of silence,
I leave the only tracks.

We have walked far enough, the dog and I, and so we turn around. It is good to watch a storm roll in when hearth and home are only a few easy miles down the trail.

Make yourself at home,
said the mountain, so the clouds
lay down for the night.

The Man Who Slept with a Bear

He had always wanted to see what the inside of a bear den looked like. It was well into November when he thought he saw some diggings about half way up the north slope of a canyon on the edge of town. He scoped it out with his binoculars. Sure looked like the real deal. Maybe his time had come. So he walked up through some ponderosas and Douglas fir, passed a large pile of bear scat, mostly grass, that looked like it had been around for a while. He sat down by some large granite boulders that had been dislodged underneath a rocky overhang, below which was a small opening, barely big enough to shimmy through on his belly. Above the opening he could see the tell-tale claw marks in the dirt where the bear had been digging. It being late November—the early days of hibernation season before the bears have slipped into a deeper torpor—only a fool would linger here. He poked his head into the portal's entry way and shimmied in even farther. A splash of daylight cast a glow on what appeared to be the back wall of the den. The tunnel wasn't that deep. It went in maybe eight feet or so. Since he could see all the way in to the back wall of this hole and since he didn't notice any sign of life, he kept going. He felt a surge of adrenalin, a welcome jolt since lately he'd been feeling a little sluggish. He'd been putting on weight and his afternoon naps had been getting longer and longer. The farther in he went, the wider the tunnel became until there was enough space to crawl on his knees and turn around. At the end of the tunnel, there appeared to be a space dug into the side of the wall but he couldn't see how far back it went. He lay down on the shredded bark of a Douglas fir which the bear had piled up on the floor of the den for a little added comfort. The smell of the bark was pleasing, but there was another lingering odor that he couldn't identify. He looked back toward the glow of the entrance and closed his eyes as he imagined himself entering into the depths of a very long sleep. He began to feel a little drowsy. He had to admit, the idea of hibernating for a while had its appeal. Maybe by the time he emerged, the pandemic would have played itself out. And then the great hairy limbs of the bear came out of the shadows, and wrapped around him from behind, sharp claws pressing firmly into his belly. Somehow he had the wherewithal not to yell, not to try and bolt. Those claws, after all, could have torn out his entrails in an instant. Instead, he just played dead. He played dead for a long time. He played dead till the light at the entrance to the cave disappeared. Till night had come. Till he could not stay awake any longer. He woke up in total darkness. He wasn't sure if it was the same night. He realized the bear was spooning him, its big head breathing hard right behind his. The bear's breath was the odor he had noticed earlier. Up close it was strong, a hint of rosehip maybe, but mostly fishy and slightly putrid. It occurred to him that this was the sow that he had been seeing for years, the one who had produced numerous cubs until she didn't anymore, the one who had broken into his house once and raided his refrigerator. Maybe she just wanted some company. And who was he to argue? She had him where she wanted him and, truth be told, it was kind of cozy in there. He figured there would come a time in a matter of weeks or months when she would emerge from her den. Maybe then he would make a break for it, but not until then. Not with those claws firmly implanted in the soft flesh of his belly. And so he went into a very deep sleep. And his dreams were bear dreams. He climbed a snowfield on the side of the mountain and slid down on his belly. He noodled a big rainbow trout out of a creek and ate it raw. He gorged himself on raspberries and lay in the sun. He wallowed in some muddy flats next to a lake on a hot summer day. And he dreamed—at least he thought he was dreaming—that he went out on a full moon ramble, occasionally sitting up on his haunches to sniff at a breeze that was drifting through the aspens.

Riding the Wheel

Riding the Wheel

Since the cranes appear in late February and are gone by the time the vultures arrive in early April, since the aspens will leaf out a few weeks later and the warblers will find shelter there, since the wind will blow till most of the snow is gone from the high peaks and the meadowlarks offer their lilting serenade from valley cottonwoods, since the creeks will rise as the sun tracks north toward its solstice, since the swallows and nighthawks will swoop through the end-of-day sky chasing the smaller winged ones, since a river of bats will emerge every evening from the old mine up north to do the same, since the bluebirds will be hatching and minding their young ones, since thunderheads trailing veils of rain will drift across the valley on July afternoons, since the blue columbines will grace the edges of talus slopes and boulder fields up high, since valley meadows will go yellow with black-eyed susans and purple with the blooms of asters and beeplants, since the sun will settle into a more southerly path, rendering the light a little softer on August afternoons, since the hummingbirds will leave on their impossibly long flight to Central and South America, since the hermit thrush will add a few more ethereal refrains in the last light of an Indian summer evening before joining the great wave of songbirds headed south, since only the regulars—nuthatches, juncos, chickadees, and jays among them—will fill this hillside with their presence while the dippers flash through the riffles of the creeks in the canyons, since the elk will be bugling for their mates as the snowline descends from the high ridges, since whirling showers of yellow aspen leaves will be released to the wind, since the bears will forage through remnant patches of rosehips and chokecherries, since southbound cranes will fly out of low autumn clouds, pausing for a few weeks to glean the grain left behind from valley harvests, since the first flurries of snow will drift across the lower reaches of the higher elevations where the ptarmigans have all gone white and the snowline will continue its descent until the first storm arrives, since the real cold days will come and go—mostly come—along with longer nights and a deepening silence, since the winds of spring will eventually begin to stir again, the cranes will reappear, and we will notice the big wheel of life turning (even though it's turning all the time as the constellations remind us) and the sequence of events herein described will likely happen again, one might imagine time as a circular phenomenon, although it might also be that this is just a label which helps us make sense of things, that time is really just a shapeless medium through which everything moves, but speculations about the nature of time are best left to those who really understand such things; what I will say, what I can say for sure, is that I will join with those whose calendar looks more like a circle than a line and I will pledge my allegiance to the big wheel of life which, among other things, brings the western tanagers back to the pinyon just beyond this window right about now, and which offers some hope, even in these precarious times, that what has been will be again.

About the Author

Peter Anderson's other books include *Reading Colorado: A Literary Road Guide,* an anthology of place-based writings; *Heading Home: Field Notes,* a collection of flash prose and prose poems exploring rural life and the modern day eccentricities of the American West; and *First Church of the Higher Elevations,* a collection of essays on wildness, mountain places, and the life of the spirit. He lives with his family on the western slope of the Sangre de Cristo Mountains in southern Colorado where he edited and published *Pilgrimage Magazine,* served as poetry editor for the *Mountain Gazette,* taught writing at Adams State University, wrote a column for *Colorado Central Magazine* called "Dispatch from the Edge," and launched the Crestone Poetry Festival (poemfest.com), an annual gathering of southwestern poets.

For more information on his work, check out:
petehowardanderson.com

www.ingramcontent.com/pod-product-compliance
Lightning Source LLC
Chambersburg PA
CBHW030916170426
43193CB00009BA/872